Introduction

Everyone uses pot holders—they're useful, versatile and can be made with fabric scraps and leftover cotton batting! Brighten up your kitchen by quickly stitching a set. Stitch a couple extras to give away, and you will be ready with a much-appreciated gift.

All the pot holders in this book are fun to stitch, using mostly beginner and easy blocks. The colourful array of designs will inspire you to start quilting today!

Table of Contents

General Instructions

Basic Tools & Supplies

Specific fabrics and pieces needed are listed for each pot holder; however, there are basic tools, supplies and materials that are needed to finish the pieced blocks into pot holders. Below is a list of tools and supplies needed for each pot holder.

Fabrics

Use tightly woven, 100 per cent cotton fabric in the colours listed or in your own choice of colours for all piecing and appliqué.

Backing Fabric

A 100 per cent cotton backing piece should be cut 1" larger all around than the finished block.

Batting

One layer of regular batting does not work in pot holders. The pot holders in this book each have three layers of cotton batting. The batting is cut the same size as the backing. You may purchase heat-resistant batting, if desired.

Hanging Ring

A 1" plastic ring is stitched to the top corner of each of the pot holders in this book.

Thread

You will need a neutral-coloured cotton thread for piecing each block. Clear nylon monofilament should not be used in pot holders because it can melt with high heat.

You will need either matching or contrasting quilting thread, depending on whether or not you want your stitches to show.

Template Material

Instructions are given for using templates later, but you will need template material to create patterns for cutting pieces.

Fine-Tip Permanent Marker

Use this marker to trace around the templates on the wrong side of the fabrics.

Fusible Web

Fusible web is a paper-backed fusible product that is applied to the wrong side of appliqué shapes, and then is used to bond the shapes to the fabrics. It is used when machine-appliqué methods are recommended.

Chalk Pencil or Fine Lead Pencil

These marking tools are used to trace patterns on template material and to transfer embroidery or appliqué detail lines to the templates and fabric.

Basic Sewing Tools

Needles, pins, shears, scissors, ruler, rotary cutter and mat, and other basic sewing tools may be needed.

Basic Technique Instructions

Basic piecing and appliqué techniques are used to complete the pot holders. This simple review of the techniques should help a beginner with questions.

Making Templates

All piecing and appliqué templates are given at the end of the book.

To create a template, place the template material over the printed page, and trace the shape using a fine-tip permanent marker. Transfer the grain-line arrows to the piece. Add the label to the template.

Place all traced templates together in a folder or envelope and label for future use.

Cutting Fabric for Piecing

Place the prepared template right side down on the wrong side of selected fabric referring to grain-line placement marked on the template as shown in Figure 1; trace around edges using a fine-tip permanent marker, referring to project instructions for number and colour to cut. Cut out shapes on marked lines.

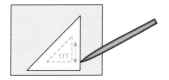

Figure 1

Piecing

Machine-piecing is recommended for all patterns in this book. Set your machine stitch length from 10–12 stitches per inch or 2.5–3.

All seam allowances are ¼" and are included in piecing templates and pieces listed in the cutting instructions provided with each pattern.

To join pieces, pin two pieces right sides together with edges aligned, and stitch from one end to the other using a ¼" seam allowance.

Partial Seams

Many of the blocks include adding pieces using partial seams. This method is often used to frame the centre or outside of the block. The piece being added may be an unpieced or pieced strip.

To begin a partial seam, match one end of the piece being added to the unit it will be stitched to; stitch along the length to within 1" of the end of the unit being stitched to as shown in Figure 2. Press the seam as directed with the pattern, normally toward the piece being added as shown in Figure 3.

Figure 2   **Figure 3**

Pin and stitch the second piece being added to the stitched end of the previously stitched unit as shown in Figure 4; press.

Figure 4

Continue adding strips until you reach the starting side with the partial seam; complete sewing the loose end to complete the partial seam as shown in Figure 5 and press.

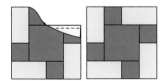

Figure 5

Appliqué

Appliqué shapes are added on top of pieced sections or plain pieces.

Hand-appliquéd pieces are lightly traced on the right side of the fabric using a chalk pencil or fine lead pencil. Cut around traced patterns, adding a ⅛"–¼" seam allowance all around when cutting.

To stitch in place, fold edges under to the marked lines as you stitch the piece to the background using thread to match the fabric, referring to Figure 6.

Figure 6

To make curved edges lie flat, cut slits, perpendicular to the marked line, into the seam allowance, as shown in Figure 7.

Figure 7

Using a sharp needle and a 12"–18" length of thread, turn the edge under at the marked line and stitch to the background. Do not turn under edges of pieces where they are overlapped by other pieces.

For fusible machine appliqué, you will need to purchase fusible web. Reverse patterns and trace onto the paper side of the fusible web; then cut out, leaving a margin around each one. Fuse the paper shape to the wrong side of fabrics as directed on patterns for number and colour to cut; cut out shapes on traced lines. Remove paper backing.

Arrange the appliqué shape on the background, and fuse in place referring to the manufacturer's instructions.

Using a machine zigzag or satin stitch, stitch around the edges of the piece with matching or contrasting thread.

Finishing the Pot Holders

Layer a completed block with backing and batting squares or rectangles 1" larger all around; pin or baste layers together to hold flat.

Quilt by hand or machine using quilting thread to match or contrast with fabrics. Most of the pot holders in this book were machine-quilted in the ditch of seams between the pieces.

When quilting is complete, trim the batting and backing edges even with the pieced block.

A length and colour suggestion for the binding is listed with each pot-holder design. Press this length of binding in half along the length with wrong sides together to make a double-layered strip.

Pin the raw edge of the binding strip to the raw edge of the right side of the pot holder, leaving 4" at the beginning loose as shown in Figure 8.

Figure 8

Stitch to within ¼" of one corner; leaving the needle in the fabric, turn and sew diagonally to the corner as shown in Figure 9.

Figure 9

Fold the binding at a 45-degree angle up and away from the pot holder as shown in Figure 10 and back down even with the raw edge of the next side.

Figure 10

Starting at the top raw edge of the pot holder, begin sewing the next side as shown in Figure 11. Repeat at the next three corners.

Figure 11

As you approach the beginning of the binding strip, stop stitching and overlap the binding ends ½" as shown in Figure 12; trim. Join the two ends with a ¼" seam allowance, and press the seam open. Reposition the joined binding strip along the edge, and resume stitching to the beginning.

Figure 12

Press the binding strip up and away from the pot holder on the right side; turn to the back side, and hand-stitch in place, mitring the corners on the back side as shown in Figure 13.

Figure 13

Through the Window

Designs by Trice Boerens

Make a set of pot holders with a stained-glass look using blue and yellow fabrics.

Notes

Cut pieces as listed either using a rotary cutter and rotary ruler, or using the templates which start on page 46.

Refer to the General Instructions (see pages 2–4) for a list of basic sewing supplies and tools needed and for instructions to finish your pot holders.

Refer to the Piecing Diagram given with each block for assembly ideas.

Sun & Sky

Skill Level
Beginner

Fabric & Piece Requirements
2 S3 yellow solid

3 S3 cream print

4 S3 turquoise tonal

6—1" x 2½" A purple print

2—1" x 7½" B purple print

4—1" x 8" C purple print

1—2" x 36" strip gold print for binding

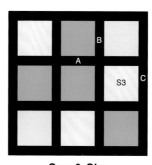

Sun & Sky
Placement Diagram
8" x 8"

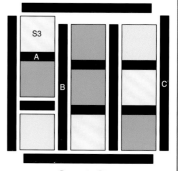

Sun & Sky
Piecing Diagram

Instructions

Arrange and join the S3 squares with A in three rows of three squares each; press seams toward A.

Join the rows with B; press seams toward B to complete the pieced centre.

Sew C to each side of the pieced centre using a partial seam, referring to the General Instructions (see page 3) to complete the pieced block.

Windowpanes

Skill Level
Beginner

Fabric & Piece Requirements

18 S9 each purple print and turquoise tonal

6—1" x 2½" A lavender tonal

2—1" x 7½" B lavender tonal

4—1" x 8" C lavender tonal

1—2" x 36" strip green print for binding

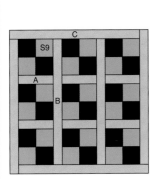

Windowpanes
Placement Diagram
8" x 8"

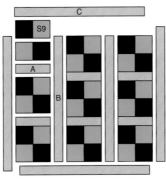

Windowpanes
Piecing Diagram

Instructions

Sew a turquoise S9 to a purple S9; press seams toward darker fabric. Repeat to make 18 S9 units.

Join two S9 units to make a Four-Patch unit referring to Figure 1; press seam in one direction. Repeat to make nine Four-Patch units.

Figure 1

Join three Four-Patch units with two A pieces to make a row; press seams toward A. Repeat to make three rows.

Join the rows with B; press seams toward B to complete the pieced centre.

Sew C to each side of the pieced centre using a partial seam, referring to the General Instructions (see page 3) to complete the pieced block.

Afternoon Shadows

Skill Level

Easy

Fabric & Piece Requirements

9 T7 triangles each lavender tonal and purple print

6—1" x 2½" A cream tonal

2—1" x 7½" B cream tonal

4—1" x 8" C cream tonal

1—2" x 36" strip green print for binding

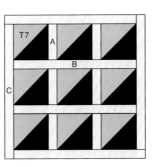

Afternoon Shadows
Placement Diagram
8" x 8"

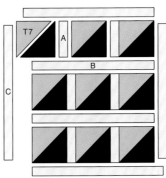

Afternoon Shadows
Piecing Diagram

Instructions

Sew a lavender T7 to a purple T7 along the diagonal; press seams toward darker fabric. Repeat to make nine T7 units.

Join three T7 units with two A pieces to make a row; press seams toward A. Repeat to make three rows.

Join the rows with B; press seams toward B to complete the pieced centre.

Sew C to each side of the pieced centre using a partial seam, referring to the General Instructions (see page 3) to complete the pieced block.

Through the Window

West Winds

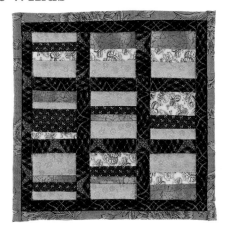

Skill Level

Beginner

Fabric & Piece Requirements

Assorted coordinating scraps cut into 3"-long strips in varying widths from ½"–1½" wide

6—1" x 2½" B purple print

2—1" x 7½" C purple print

4—1" x 8" D purple print

1—2" x 36" strip blue print for binding

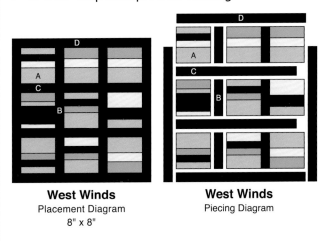

West Winds
Placement Diagram
8" x 8"

West Winds
Piecing Diagram

Instructions

Referring to Figure 2, join a variety of scrap strips and square to 3" x 3" to make a scrappy A square; press seams in one direction. Repeat to make nine scrappy A squares.

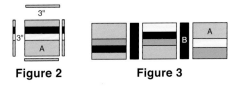

Figure 2   **Figure 3**

Referring to Figure 3, join three scrappy A squares with two B pieces to make a row; press seams toward B. Repeat to make three rows.

Join the rows with C; press seams toward C to complete the pieced centre.

Sew D to each side of the pieced centre using a partial seam, referring to the General Instructions (see page 3) to complete the pieced block.

Bluebird Quartet

Skill Level

Beginner

Fabric & Piece Requirements

2 S3 each blue mottled and turquoise tonal

8 S9 each blue mottled and turquoise tonal

16—1½" x 2½" A yellow print

1—2" x 36" strip yellow print for binding

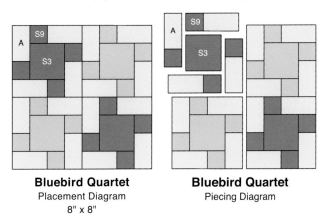

Bluebird Quartet
Placement Diagram
8" x 8"

Bluebird Quartet
Piecing Diagram

Instructions

Sew a blue S9 square to A to make an A-S9 unit; press seam toward A. Repeat to make eight each blue and turquoise A-S9 units.

Match the S9 end of an A-S9 unit to one end of a matching S3 square, and stitch to within 1" of the end of S3 to make a partial seam as shown in Figure 4; press seam away from S3.

Figure 4

Continue adding A-S9 units around S3 and complete the partial seam to complete a block quarter; press seams away from S3. Repeat to make two each matching block quarters.

Join one each-colour block quarter to make a row; press seams toward blue block quarters. Repeat to make two rows.

Join the rows to complete the pieced block.

Lovebirds

Skill Level
Beginner

Fabric & Piece Requirements
2 S3 blue mottled

4 S3 each lavender and gold solids

8 S9 blue mottled

8—1½" x 2½" A yellow print

1—2" x 36" strip yellow print for binding

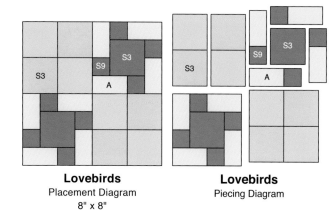

Lovebirds
Placement Diagram
8" x 8"

Lovebirds
Piecing Diagram

Instructions

Complete two blue mottled block quarters referring to Figures 4 and 5, and steps from Bluebird Quartet.

Figure 5

Sew a lavender S3 to a gold S3 to make an S3 unit referring to Figure 6; press seam toward darker fabric. Repeat to make four S3 units.

Figure 6

Join two S3 units to make a Four-Patch unit referring to Figure 7; press seam in one direction. Repeat to make two Four-Patch units.

Figure 7

Join one Four-Patch unit and one block quarter to make a row; press seams toward the Four-Patch unit. Repeat to make two rows.

Join the rows to complete the pieced block. ■

Creative Cook

Designs by Trice Boerens

Many quilt blocks have food-related names, which makes them perfect designs for pot holders.

Notes

Cut pieces as listed either using a rotary cutter and rotary ruler, or using the templates which start on page 46.

Refer to the General Instructions (see pages 2–4) for a list of basic sewing supplies and tools needed, and for instructions to finish your pot holders.

Refer to the Piecing Diagram given with each block for assembly ideas.

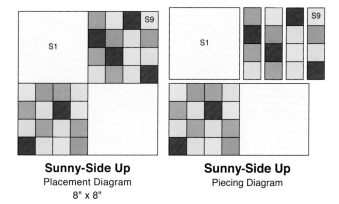

Sunny-Side Up
Placement Diagram
8" x 8"

Sunny-Side Up
Piecing Diagram

Instructions

Join four S9 squares to make a row; repeat to make eight rows. Press seams in one direction.

Join four S9 rows to make an S9 unit, alternating direction of seams in rows; press seams in one direction. Repeat to make two S9 units.

Sew an S9 unit to S1 to make a row; press seam toward S1. Repeat to make two rows.

Join the rows to complete the pieced top; press seam in one direction.

Sunny-Side Up

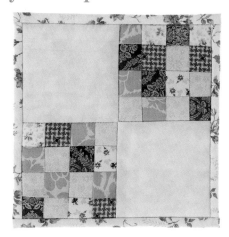

Skill Level

Easy

Fabric & Piece Requirements

2 S1 peach mottled

32 S9 assorted fabrics

1—2" x 36" strip cream print for binding

Dessert Party

Skill Level

Easy

Fabric & Piece Requirements

2 S1 cream print

2 S3 dark rose print

8 S9 dark rose print

8—1½" x 2½" A pink tonal

1—2" x 36" strip tan print for binding

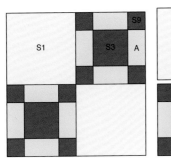

Dessert Party
Placement Diagram
8" x 8"

Dessert Party
Piecing Diagram

Instructions

Sew S9 to opposite ends of A; repeat to make four A-S9 units. Press seams toward S9.

Sew A to opposite sides of S3; press seams toward S3. Repeat to make two A-S3 units.

Sew an A-S9 unit to opposite sides of an A-S3 unit to complete an A-S unit; press seams toward the A-S3 unit. Repeat to make two A-S units.

Sew S1 to an A-S unit to make a row; press seam toward S1. Repeat to make two row units. Join the rows to complete the pieced top; press seam in one direction.

Pink Lemonade

Skill Level

Easy

Fabric & Piece Requirements

16 S9 pink tonal

20 S9 green print

1 S3 green leaf print

4 S3 cream tonal

4—1½" x 2½" A pink tonal

20" length ½"-wide pink rickrack

1—2" x 36" strip gold print for binding

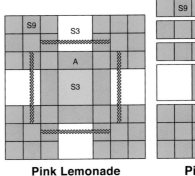

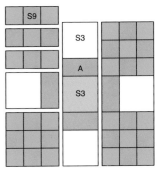

Pink Lemonade
Placement Diagram
8" x 8"

Pink Lemonade
Piecing Diagram

Instructions

Referring to Figure 1, sew a pink S9 between two green S9s; press seams toward the centre square. Repeat to make eight units.

Make 8

Make 4

Figure 1

Sew a green S9 between two pink S9s, again referring to Figure 1; press seams away from the centre square. Repeat to make four units.

Figure 2

Sew a pink/green/pink S9 unit between two green/pink/green S9 units to complete a Nine-Patch unit as shown in Figure 2; press seams toward the centre unit. Repeat to make four Nine-Patch units.

Sew A to opposite sides of the green S3; press seams toward A. Add a cream S3 to each A side to complete the centre row; press seams toward S3.

Sew A to one end of each remaining cream S3 to make two side units; press seams toward A.

Sew a side unit between two Nine-Patch units to make a side row; press seams toward the side unit. Repeat to make two side rows.

Sew the centre row between the two side rows; press seams toward the centre row.

Cut the pink rickrack into four 5" pieces.

Unpick the seams between the centre green and inside pink S9 squares as shown in Figure 3.

Figure 3   **Figure 4**

Insert a piece of rickrack into the seam between units all around as shown in Figure 4; when satisfied with placement, stitch rickrack in place.

Re-stitch seams to complete the pieced top.

Supper Time

Skill Level
Easy

Fabric & Piece Requirements
1 S3 each pink and orange tonals, and green and purple prints

4 S3 cream tonal

2 S9 each cream solid and cream print

5 S9 each pink and orange tonals, and green and purple prints

8 S9 cream tonal

1—2" x 36" strip peach print for binding

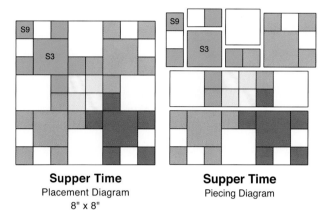

Supper Time
Placement Diagram
8" x 8"

Supper Time
Piecing Diagram

Instructions

Sew a pink S9 to a cream tonal S9; press seam toward darker fabric. Repeat to make two units; add a pink S9 to the cream end of one unit; press seams toward darker fabric.

Sew the pink/cream S9 to one side of the pink S3; press seam toward S3. Sew the pink/cream/pink S9 unit to the adjacent side of S3 to complete a corner unit as shown in Figure 5; press seams away from S3.

Figure 5

Repeat steps to make one each purple, green and orange corner unit.

Sew a pink S9 to a green S9 to make a pink/green unit; repeat to make one each pink/purple, orange/purple and green/orange units; press seams toward darker fabrics.

Sew these units to one end of each cream S3 to make side units as shown in Figure 6; press seams toward S3.

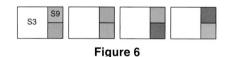

Figure 6

Sew a cream solid S9 to a cream print S9; repeat. Press seams toward the print square. Join the two units to complete the centre unit; press seam in one direction.

Arrange and join the pieced units in rows referring to the Piecing Diagram; press seams in one direction.

Biscuit Baskets

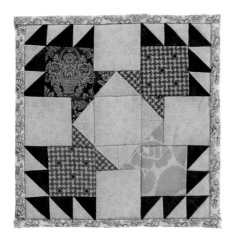

Skill Level

Intermediate

Fabric & Piece Requirements

2 T4 each purple, green and dark rose prints, and orange tonal

20 T4 purple mottled

28 T4 pink tonal

1 S3 each purple, green and dark rose prints, and orange tonal

5 S3 pink tonal

1—2" x 36" strip white print for binding

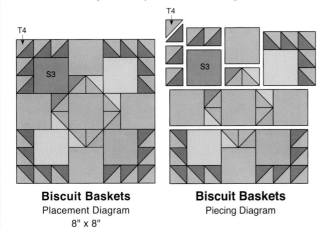

Biscuit Baskets
Placement Diagram
8" x 8"

Biscuit Baskets
Piecing Diagram

Instructions

Sew a pink T4 to each different-colour T4 to make T units; press seams away from the pink T4 triangles.

Join two pink/purple mottled T units as shown in Figure 7; press seam in one direction. Repeat to make four units.

Figure 7

Sew a unit to one side of each orange, green, purple print and dark rose S3 square as shown in Figure 8; press seams toward S3.

Join three pink/purple mottled T units, again referring to Figure 7; press seams in one direction. Repeat to make four units.

Sew a unit to the adjacent sides of the previously pieced unit to complete the corner units as shown in Figure 8; press seams toward S3.

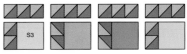

Figure 8

Join the remaining T units with pink sides touching as shown in Figure 9; press seams open. Sew these units to pink S3 squares, again referring to Figure 9; press seams toward S3.

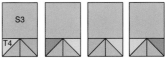

Figure 9

Arrange and join the pieced units in rows referring to the Piecing Diagram; press seams in adjacent rows in opposite directions.

Join the rows to complete the pieced top; press seams in one direction. ∎

Falling Leaves

Designs by Trice Boerens

Introduce some appliqué and embroidery to your quilted pot holders with these leaf designs.

Notes

Cut pieces as listed either using a rotary cutter and rotary ruler, or using the templates which start on page 46.

Refer to the General Instructions (see pages 2–4) for a list of basic sewing supplies and tools needed, and for instructions to finish your pot holders.

Refer to the Piecing Diagram given with each block for assembly ideas.

Green Leaf

Skill Level

Easy

Fabric & Piece Requirements

1 S10 brown solid

Assorted coordinating scraps cut into 3"-long strips in varying widths from ½"–2" wide for A

4—1" x 5¼" B green plaid

4—1½" x 2¾" C brown solid

Scrap light green mottled for appliqué

1—2" x 36" strip burgundy print for binding

Light green embroidery floss

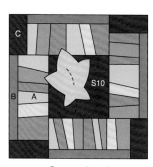

Green Leaf
Placement Diagram
8" x 8"

Green Leaf
Piecing Diagram

Instructions

Referring to Figure 1, join a variety of scrap strips to make an A row; trim the A row to 2¼" x 5¼". Repeat to make four A rows.

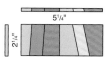

Figure 1

Sew B to one long side of each A row; press seam toward B. Repeat to make four A-B units.

Sew C to one end of each A-B unit to complete a side unit; press seams toward C.

Sew a side unit to each side of S10 using a partial seam, referring to the General Instructions (see page 3) to complete the pieced centre; press seams toward the side units.

Cut and prepare green leaf motif using template given on page 45, and appliqué to the pieced block, referring to the General Instructions (see page 3) and the Placement Diagram.

Stem-stitch leaf vein and stem using 2 strands light green embroidery floss.

Oak Leaf

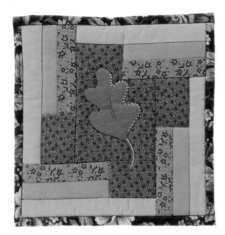

Skill Level
Easy

Fabric & Piece Requirements
1 S10 violet print

4—2" x 2½" A violet print

4—1¼" x 4½" each grey print B and lavender solid C

4—1¼" x 6¼" D tan solid

Scrap dark orange solid for leaf appliqué

1—2" x 36" strip burgundy print for binding

Light grey and rust embroidery floss

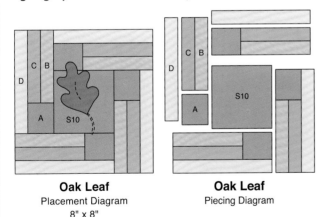

Oak Leaf
Placement Diagram
8" x 8"

Oak Leaf
Piecing Diagram

Instructions
Sew B to C along the length; press seam toward B. Repeat to make four B-C units.

Add A to one end of each B-C unit; press seams toward A.

Add D to each A-B-C unit; press seams toward D.

Sew the A-B-C-D units to S10 using a partial seam, referring to the General Instructions (see page 3); press seams away from S10.

Cut and prepare oak leaf motif using template given on page 45, and appliqué to the pieced block, referring to the General Instructions (see page 3) and the Placement Diagram.

Stem-stitch leaf vein and one stem using 2 strands rust embroidery floss; stem-stitch second leaf stem and buttonhole-stitch along right-hand side of leaf using two strands light grey embroidery floss to complete the block.

Fall Walk
Skill Level
Easy

Fabric & Piece Requirements
1 S10 brown print

4 T9 each tan and brown prints

4—1¼" x 4½" each rose print A and cream tonal B

4—1¼" x 6¼" C violet print

1—2" x 36" strip cream print for binding

Instructions

Sew a tan T9 to a brown T9 along the diagonal; press seam toward darker fabric. Repeat to make four T9 units.

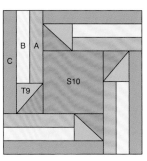

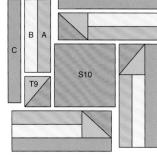

Fall Walk
Placement Diagram
8" x 8"

Fall Walk
Piecing Diagram

Sew A to B along the length; press seam toward A. Repeat to make four A-B units.

Add a T9 unit to one end of each A-B unit; press seams toward A-B.

Add C to each A-B-T9 unit to make side units; press seams toward C.

Sew the side units to S10 using a partial seam, referring to the General Instructions (see page 3); press seams away from S10. ■

Town Square

Designs by Trice Boerens

Centre units are framed with triangles or strips in these colourful pot holders.

Notes

Cut pieces as listed either using a rotary cutter and rotary ruler, or using the templates which start on page 46.

Refer to the General Instructions (see pages 2–4) for a list of basic sewing supplies and tools needed, and for instructions to finish your pot holders.

Refer to the Piecing Diagram given with each block for assembly ideas.

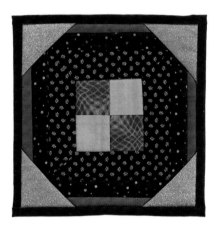

Evening Walk

Skill Level

Easy

Fabric & Piece Requirements

2 S8 each green tonal and blue solid

4 T2 tan tonal

4—1¾" x 7" A navy print

4—1¼" x 5¾" B red print

4—1" x 5¾" C green solid

1—2" x 36" strip burgundy solid for binding

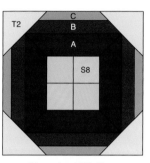

Evening Walk
Placement Diagram
8" x 8"

Evening Walk
Piecing Diagram

Instructions

Sew a blue S8 to a green S8; repeat. Press seam toward darker fabric.

Join the two S8 units to complete the block centre as shown in Figure 1; press seam in one direction.

Figure 1

Centre and sew an A strip on each side of the block centre, mitring corners; press seams toward A. ***Note:*** *Refer to the General Instructions (see page 4) for making mitred corner seams.*

Sew a B strip to a C strip; press seam toward C. Repeat to make four B-C strips.

Trim each end of the B-C strips at a 45-degree angle as shown in Figure 2.

Figure 2

Sew a trimmed strip to each side of the pieced centre.

Sew T2 to each corner to complete the block; press seams toward T2.

Town Square

Green Space

Skill Level

Easy

Fabric & Piece Requirements

2 S8 each green tonal and blue solid

4 T2 red print

4—1¼" x 6" A yellow print

4—1¼" x 5¾" B green solid

4—1½" x 6½" C pumpkin solid

1—2" x 36" strip burgundy solid for binding

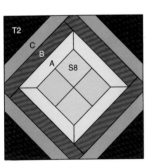

Green Space
Placement Diagram
8" x 8"

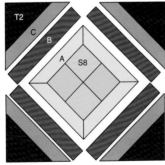

Green Space
Piecing Diagram

Instructions

Sew a blue S8 to a green S8; repeat. Press seams toward darker fabric. Join the two S8 units to complete the block centre; press seam in one direction.

Centre and sew an A strip on each side of the block centre, mitring corners; press seams toward A. ***Note: Refer to the General Instructions (see page 4) for making mitred corner seams.***

Sew a B strip to each side using a partial seam, referring to the General Instructions (see page 3); press seams toward B.

Centre and sew a C strip to T2 as shown in Figure 3; press seam toward T2. Trim C even with edges of T2, again referring to Figure 3. Repeat to make four C-T2 units.

Figure 3

Sew a C-T2 unit to each side of the pieced unit; press seams toward the C-T2 units.

Trim the B strips even with the edges of the C-T2 units as shown in Figure 4 to complete the block.

Figure 4

Brass Band

Skill Level

Easy

Fabric & Piece Requirements

2 S5 each red and white/red prints

4 T10 each cream tonal and tan print

4 T8 black print

4—2⅝" x 4" A black check

1—2" x 36" strip burgundy tonal for binding

Instructions

Sew a red S5 to a white/red S5; press seam toward darker fabric. Repeat to make two units.

Join the two S5 units to complete the centre unit; press seam in one direction.

Sew T8 to each end of A; press seam toward T8. Repeat to make two A-T8 units.

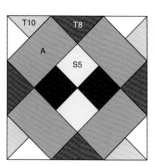

Brass Band
Placement Diagram
8" x 8"

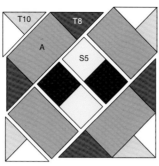

Brass Band
Piecing Diagram

Sew a cream T10 to a tan T10; press seam toward darker fabric. Repeat to make four T10 units.

Sew a T10 unit to an A-T8 unit to complete a corner unit as shown in Figure 5; press seam toward the T10 unit. Repeat to make two corner units.

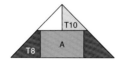

Figure 5

Sew A to opposite sides of the S5 centre unit; press seams toward A. Add a T10 unit to each A end to complete the centre row, referring to Figure 6; press seams toward A.

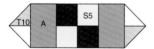

Figure 6

Sew a corner unit to opposite sides of the centre row to complete the pieced block; press seams toward corner units.

Town Fathers

Skill Level
Easy

Fabric & Piece Requirements
2 T3 each red print and green solid
4—2¼" x 5" A yellow print
4—2¼" x 5" B black print
1—2" x 36" strip black dot for binding

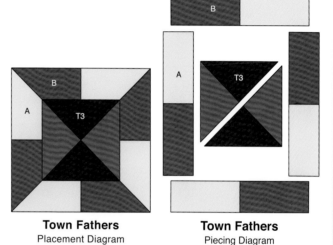

Town Fathers
Placement Diagram
8" x 8"

Town Fathers
Piecing Diagram

Instructions
Sew a red T3 to a green T3 as shown in Figure 7; press seam toward the darker fabric. Repeat to make two T3 units.

Figure 7

Join the T3 units as shown in Figure 8 to complete the block centre; press seam in one direction.

Figure 8

Sew A to B on the short ends; press seam toward the darker fabric. Repeat to make four A-B units.

Centre and sew an A-B unit to each side of the block centre, mitring corners, referring to the General Instructions (see page 3) to complete the pieced block. ■

English Garden

Designs by Trice Boerens

Blocks with flower colours create a fabric garden in these ladylike pot holders.

Notes

Cut pieces as listed either using a rotary cutter and rotary ruler, or using the templates which start on page 46.

Refer to the General Instructions (see pages 2–4) for a list of basic sewing supplies and tools needed, and for instructions to finish your pot holders.

Refer to the Piecing Diagram given with each block for assembly ideas.

End of the Path

Skill Level
Beginner

Fabric & Piece Requirements
1 S3 green tonal

2—1½" x 3½" each light A and dark B scraps

2—1½" x 5½" each light C and dark D scraps

2—1½" x 7½" each light E and dark F scraps

1—2" x 36" strip purple print for binding

Instructions
Sew pieces around S3 in alphabetical order, starting at bottom of square and working counterclockwise, and using a partial seam at the beginning of each round, referring to the General Instructions (see page 3) to complete the pieced block; press seam toward the most recently added strip as you sew.

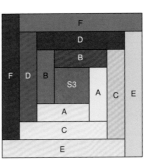

End of the Path
Placement Diagram
8" x 8"

End of the Path
Piecing Diagram

Amazing

Skill Level
Easy

Fabric & Piece Requirements
2 S3 each 2 different green tonals

4 each 1½" x 3½" light A and B scraps

4 each 1½" x 3½" dark C and D scraps

1—2" x 36" strip purple print for binding

Instructions
Sew strips to S3 squares in alphabetical order using a partial seam at the beginning of each round, referring to the General Instructions (see page 3) to complete four S3 units; press seam toward the most recently added strip as you sew.

English Garden

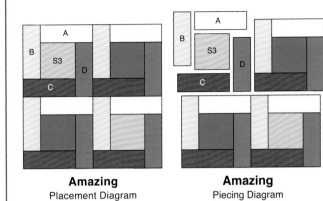

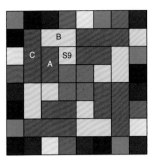

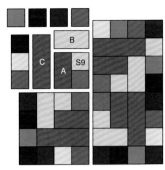

| **Amazing**
Placement Diagram
8" x 8" | **Amazing**
Piecing Diagram | **Violet Patches**
Placement Diagram
8" x 8" | **Violet Patches**
Piecing Diagram |

Join two S3 units to make a row; press seam in one direction. Repeat to make two rows.

Join the rows to complete the pieced block; press seam in one direction.

Violet Patches

Skill Level
Easy

Fabric & Piece Requirements
4 S9 each gold and green tonals

28 S9 assorted colours

4—1½" x 2½" each purple print A and gold tonal B

4—1½" x 3½" C purple print

1—2" x 36" strip purple print for binding

Instructions
Join one each green and gold S9; press seam toward darker fabric.

Add A to the S9 unit; press seam toward A.

Sew B to the A-S9 unit and add C to make an A-B-C unit as shown in Figure 1; press seams toward B and then C.

| **Figure 1** | **Figure 2** |

Join three assorted S9 squares; press seams in one direction. Add to the C side of the A-B-C unit as shown in Figure 2; press seams toward C.

Join four assorted S9 squares; press seams in one direction. Add to the A-B-C unit, again referring to Figure 2 to complete a block quarter; press seam toward the S9 strip.

Repeat steps to complete four block quarters.

Arrange and join the block quarters to make two rows; press seams in rows in opposite directions. Join the rows to complete the pieced block; press seam in one direction.

Rose Arbour

Skill Level
Easy

Fabric & Piece Requirements

1 S3 cream print

8 S9 cream print

4 T11 green tonal

4—1½" x 2½" gold tonal B

8—1½" x 2½" maize solid A

1—2" x 36" strip rose print for binding

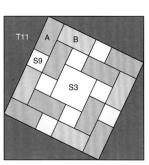

Rose Arbour
Placement Diagram
8" x 8"

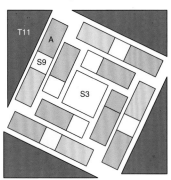

Rose Arbour
Piecing Diagram

Instructions

Sew S9 to one end of each A piece; press seams toward A.

Sew four A-S9 units to S3 using a partial seam to complete the centre unit, referring to the General Instructions (see page 3); press seams toward A-S9 units.

Sew B to the S9 end of the remaining A-S9 units; press seams toward B.

Sew the A-B-S9 strips to the centre unit using a partial seam, referring to the General Instructions (see page 3); press seams toward the A-B-S9 strips.

Sew T11 to each side of the pieced unit to complete the pieced block; press seams toward T11.

Climbing Roses

Skill Level

Easy

Fabric & Piece Requirements

4 S3 cream print

2 S9 each blue solid and blue tonal

4 S9 cream print

2—1½" x 3½" each blue solid A and blue tonal B

4—1½" x 7½" brown print C

1—2" x 36" strip green print for binding

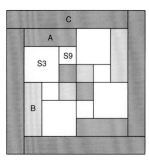

Climbing Roses
Placement Diagram
8" x 8"

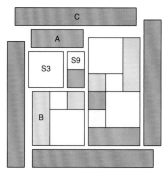

Climbing Roses
Piecing Diagram

Instructions

Sew a cream S9 to a blue solid S9; press seam toward darker fabric.

Sew the S9 unit to S3, and add blue solid A to complete a block quarter as shown in Figure 3; press seam toward S3 and A. Repeat to make two each blue solid and blue tonal block quarters.

Figure 3

Join one each blue solid and blue tonal block quarters, referring to the Piecing Diagram to make a row; press seam in one direction. Repeat to complete two rows; join the rows to complete the block centre. Press seam in one direction.

Sew a C strip to each side of the block centre using a partial seam, referring to the General Instructions (see page 3) to complete the pieced block. ■

Fresh Fruit

Designs by Trice Boerens

Appliquéd fruit makes these pot holders an appetizing addition to anyone's kitchen.

Notes

Cut pieces as listed either using a rotary cutter and rotary ruler, or using the templates which start on page 45.

Refer to the General Instructions (see pages 2–4) for a list of basic sewing supplies and tools needed, and for instructions to finish your pot holders.

Refer to the Piecing Diagram given with each block for assembly ideas.

Orange Delight

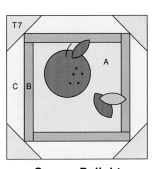

Orange Delight
Placement Diagram
8" x 8"

Orange Delight
Piecing Diagram

Instructions

Using the wrong side of A as the right side, sew B to each side of A using a partial seam, referring to the General Instructions (see page 3); press seams toward B.

Trim each end of each C strip at a 45-degree angle as shown in Figure 1.

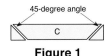

45-degree angle

C

Figure 1

Centre and sew C to each side of the A-B unit; press seams toward C.

Sew T7 to each corner to complete the pieced block.

Cut and prepare the orange and leaf motifs using templates given on page 45, and appliqué to the pieced block, referring to the General Instructions (see page 3).

Add X marks on the orange shape using 2 strands gold embroidery floss.

Stem-stitch the orange stem using 2 strands green embroidery floss to complete the block.

Skill Level

Easy

Fabric & Piece Requirements

4 T7 white/purple print

1—5½" x 5½" A orange print

4—1" x 6" B orange print

4—1½" x 6¾" C strips light blue mottled

Scraps orange and dark green solids, and green mottled for appliqué

1—2" x 36" strip orange print for binding

Gold and green embroidery floss

Fresh Fruit

Cherry Trio

Skill Level

Easy

Fabric & Piece Requirements

4 T7 yellow print

1—5½" x 5½" A yellow dot

2—1" x 5½" B white/purple print

2—1" x 6½" C white/purple print

4—1½" x 6¾" D strips light blue mottled

Scraps cherry red and leaf green solids for appliqué

1—2" x 36" strip peach print for binding

Pink and green embroidery floss

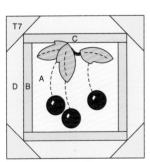

Cherry Trio
Placement Diagram
8" x 8"

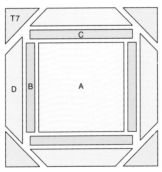

Cherry Trio
Piecing Diagram

Instructions

Sew B to opposite sides and C to the top and bottom of A; press seams toward B and C.

Trim each end of each D strip at a 45-degree angle as shown in Figure 1 of Orange Delight.

Centre and sew D to each side of the A-B-C unit; press seams toward D.

Sew T7 to each corner to complete the pieced block.

Cut and prepare the cherry and leaf motifs using templates given on page 45, and appliqué to the pieced block, referring to the General Instructions (see page 3).

Satin-stitch detail lines on the cherry shapes using 2 strands pink embroidery floss.

Satin-stitch the cherry stems and straight-stitch leaf veins using 2 strands green embroidery floss to complete the block.

Apple of Your Eye

Skill Level

Easy

Fabric & Piece Requirements

1 S7 blue solid

4 S9 gold solid

4 T7 white/purple print

4—1½" x 3½" A tan dot

2—1" x 5½" B gold check

2—1" x 6½" C gold check

4—1½" x 6¾" D cream solid

Scrap rust print for appliqué

1—2" x 36" strip white/purple print for binding

Light and dark green, and gold embroidery floss

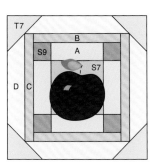

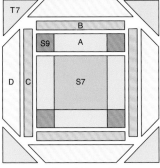

Apple of Your Eye
Placement Diagram
8" x 8"

Apple of Your Eye
Piecing Diagram

Instructions

Sew A to opposite sides of S7; press seams toward A.

Sew S9 to each end of each remaining A; press seams toward A.

Sew the A-S9 units to the remaining sides of the A-S7 unit to complete the block centre; press seams toward the A-S9 units.

Sew B to the top and bottom, and C to opposite sides of the block centre; press seams toward B and C.

Trim each end of each D strip at a 45-degree angle as in Figure 1 of Orange Delight.

Centre and sew D to each side of the block centre; press seams toward D.

Sew T7 to each corner to complete the pieced block.

Cut and prepare the apple motif using templates given on page 45, and appliqué to the pieced block, referring to the General Instructions (see page 3).

Satin-stitch detail lines on the apple shape using 2 strands gold embroidery floss.

Stem-stitch the entire leaf and leaf stem using 2 strands light and dark green embroidery floss to complete the block.

Pear Duo

Skill Level

Easy

Fabric & Piece Requirements

1 S7 light blue solid

4 S9 gold print

4 T7 white/purple print

4—1½" x 3½" A tan dot

2—1" x 5½" B light blue mottled

2—1" x 6½" C light blue mottled

4—1½" x 6¾" D yellow dot

Scraps gold solid and leaf green print for appliqué

1—2" x 36" strip white/purple print for binding

Green and turquoise embroidery floss

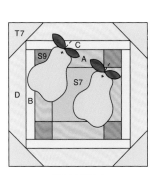

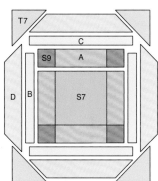

Pear Duo
Placement Diagram
8" x 8"

Pear Duo
Piecing Diagram

Instructions

Construct the block as for Apple of Your Eye block, except sew B to sides, and C to top and bottom of block centre.

Cut and prepare pear and leaf motifs using templates on page 45, and appliqué to the pieced block, referring to the General Instructions (see page 3). Add an X and stem-stitch stem on each pear, and satin-stitch around each right-hand leaf using 2 strands green embroidery floss; satin-stitch around each left-hand leaf using 2 strands turquoise embroidery floss to complete the block. ■

Spring Florals

Designs by Trice Boerens

Appliquéd flowers in pastel colours hail the arrival of spring.

Notes

Cut pieces as listed either using a rotary cutter and rotary ruler, or using the templates which start on page 44.

Refer to the General Instructions (see pages 2–4) for a list of basic sewing supplies and tools needed, and for instructions to finish your pot holders.

Refer to the Piecing Diagram given with each block for assembly ideas.

Pollination

Skill Level
Easy

Fabric & Piece Requirements
2 T10 each blue mottled and lavender tonal

4—2¾" x 3½" A cream tonal

4—2¼" x 2¾" B green tonal

4—1" x 7½" C aqua check

Scraps lavender solid and pink tonal for appliqué

1—2" x 36" strip yellow print for binding

Pink, green and blue embroidery floss

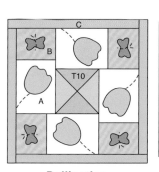
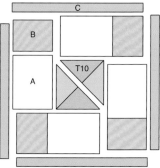

Pollination
Placement Diagram
8" x 8"

Pollination
Piecing Diagram

Instructions

Sew a blue T10 to a lavender T10; press seam toward darker fabric. Repeat to make two T10 units.

Join the T10 units to complete the block centre; press seam in one direction.

Sew B to one end of A to make a side unit; press seam toward B. Repeat to make four side units.

Sew a side unit to each side of the centre unit using a partial seam, referring to the General Instructions (see page 3); press seams toward the side units.

Sew a C strip to each side of the pieced centre using a partial seam, referring to the General Instructions (see page 3); press seams toward C.

Cut and prepare the flower and butterfly motifs using templates given on page 44, and appliqué to the pieced block, referring to the General Instructions (see page 3).

Stem-stitch flower stems using 2 strands green embroidery floss.

Stem-stitch the butterfly body and antennae using 2 strands blue embroidery floss.

Buttonhole-stitch around the flowers using 2 strands pink embroidery floss to complete the block.

Spring Florals

Pretty Posies

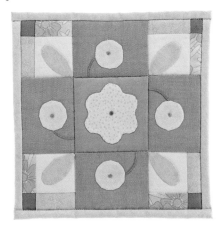

Skill Level

Easy

Fabric & Piece Requirements

4 S5 cream solid

1 S7 lavender solid

4 S6 orange solid

4—3" x 3½" A aqua solid

4—1¼" x 2¼" each pink tonal B and orange print C

Scraps light cream and light green tonals, and yellow dot for appliqué

1—2" x 36" strip tan tonal for binding

Blue and green embroidery floss

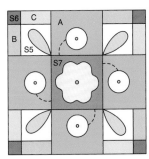

Pretty Posies
Placement Diagram
8" x 8"

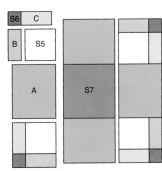

Pretty Posies
Piecing Diagram

Instructions

Sew B to one side of S5; press seam toward B. Repeat to make four B-S5 units.

Sew S6 to one end of C; press seam toward C; repeat to make four C-S6 units.

Sew a B-S5 unit to a C-S6 unit to complete a corner unit; press seams toward the C-S6 unit. Repeat to make four corner units.

Sew A to opposite sides of S7 to complete the centre row; press seams toward A.

Sew A between two corner units to complete a side row; press seams toward A. Repeat to make two side rows.

Sew the side rows to opposite sides of the centre row to complete the block piecing; press seams toward the centre row.

Cut and prepare the flower and leaf motifs using templates given on page 44, and appliqué to the pieced block, referring to the General Instructions (see page 3).

Stem-stitch flower stems using 2 strands green embroidery floss.

Satin-stitch small flower centres using 2 strands green embroidery floss; satin-stitch large flower centre using 2 strands blue embroidery floss to complete the block.

Pot of Tulips

Skill Level

Easy

Fabric & Piece Requirements

1—5¼" x 6½" A light gold tonal

2—1¼" x 1½" C light gold tonal

2—2⅛" x 2¾" E light gold tonal

1—1¼" x 4½" B purple check

1—2¾" x 3¼" D purple check

1—1¼" x 6½" F lavender print

1—1" x 6½" G purple print

1—2" x 9½" H lavender solid

Scraps lavender, and light and dark pink tonals; and pink and green solids for appliqué

1—2" x 40" strip blue print for binding

10" pink/white flowered lace trim

Blue and green embroidery floss

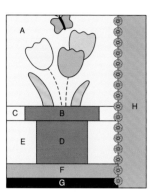 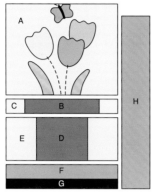

Pot of Tulips
Placement Diagram
7½" x 9"

Pot of Tulips
Piecing Diagram

Instructions

Cut and prepare the flower, butterfly and leaf motifs using templates given on page 44, and appliqué to A, referring to the General Instructions (see page 3).

Stem-stitch the flower stems using 2 strands green embroidery floss. Satin-stitch the butterfly body and antennae using 2 strands blue embroidery floss.

Sew C to each short end of B; press seams toward B.

Sew the B-C unit to A; press seam toward A.

Sew E to opposite sides of D; press seams toward E.

Sew the D-E unit to the A-B-C unit to complete the flower section; press seams toward the D-E unit.

Sew F and G to the bottom of the flower section and add H to the side edge, referring to the Piecing Diagram for positioning; press seams toward F, G and H.

Centre and stitch the lace trim over the seam between the pieced section and H to complete the block.

Pot of Blooms

Skill Level

Easy

Fabric & Piece Requirements

1—5¼" x 6½" A peach mottled

2—1¼" x 1½" C peach mottled

2—2⅛" x 2¾" E peach mottled

1—1¼" x 4½" B green tonal

1—2¾" x 3¼" D green tonal

1—1¼" x 6½" F grey print

1—1" x 6½" G aqua tonal

1—2" x 9½" H green print

Scraps lavender and blue tonals, and green mottled for appliqué

1—2" x 40" strip green tonal for binding

10" blue/white flowered lace trim

Green, purple and yellow embroidery floss

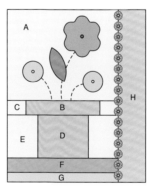 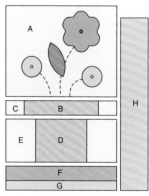

Pot of Blooms
Placement Diagram
7½" x 9"

Pot of Blooms
Piecing Diagram

Instructions

Complete the block as for Pot of Tulips using the appliqué motifs using templates given on page 44, except satin-stitch large flower centre with 2 strands purple embroidery floss and small flower centres using 2 strands yellow embroidery floss. ∎

Bright Ideas

Designs by Trice Boerens

Bright colours, especially yellow, stand out in these pot holders with framed centres.

Notes

Cut pieces as listed either using a rotary cutter and rotary ruler, or using the templates which start on page 46.

Refer to the General Instructions (see pages 2–4) for a list of basic sewing supplies and tools needed, and for instructions to finish your pot holders.

Refer to the Piecing Diagram given with each block for assembly ideas.

Lilac Square

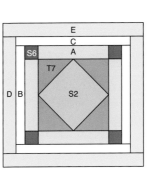

Lilac Square
Placement Diagram
8" x 8"

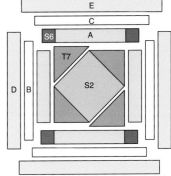

Lilac Square
Piecing Diagram

Instructions

Sew T7 to each side of S2 to complete the block centre; press seams toward T7.

Sew A to opposite sides of the block centre; press seams toward A.

Sew S6 to each end of each remaining A; press seams toward A.

Sew an A-S6 unit to the remaining sides of the block centre; press seams toward A-S6.

Sew B to opposite sides and C to the top and bottom of the block centre; press seams toward B and C. Repeat with D and E strips to complete the pieced block.

Skill Level
Easy

Fabric & Piece Requirements
1 S2 lavender solid

4 S6 purple tonal

4 T7 rust tonal

4—1¼" x 4½" A aqua solid

2—1" x 6" B cream tonal

2—1" x 7" C cream tonal

2—1¼" x 7" D yellow dot

2—1¼" x 8½" E yellow dot

1—2" x 36" strip red print for binding

Royal Blue Square

Skill Level

Easy

Fabric & Piece Requirements

1 S2 bright blue tonal

8 S9 each yellow dot and black print

4 T7 lavender solid

4—1½" x 4½" A fuchsia solid

4—1½" x 4½" B cream/purple print

1—2" x 36" strip gold solid for binding

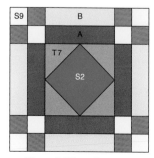

Royal Blue Square
Placement Diagram
8" x 8"

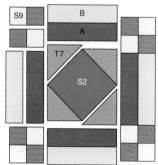

Royal Blue Square
Piecing Diagram

Instructions

Sew T7 to each side of S2 to complete the block centre; press seams toward T7.

Sew a yellow S9 to a black S9; press seam toward the darker fabric. Repeat to make eight S9 units.

Join two S9 units to make a corner unit; press seam in one direction. Repeat to make four corner units.

Sew A to B along the length; press seam toward B. Repeat to make four A-B units.

Sew an A-B unit to opposite sides of the block centre; press seams toward A-B.

Sew a corner unit to each end of each remaining A-B unit; press seams toward A-B.

Sew an A-B/corner unit to the remaining sides of the block centre to complete the pieced block; press seams away from the block centre.

Blood Orange Square

Skill Level

Easy

Fabric & Piece Requirements

1 S2 coral tonal

8 S9 each lavender solid and coral print

4 S3 orange tonal

4 T7 turquoise tonal

4—1½" x 4½" A yellow dot

1—2" x 36" strip gold solid for binding

Instructions

Sew T7 to each side of S2 to complete the block centre; press seams toward T7.

Join two each lavender and coral S9 squares to make an S9 strip; press seams toward darker fabric. Repeat to make four S9 strips.

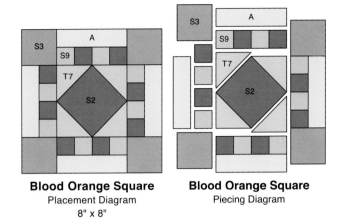

Blood Orange Square
Placement Diagram
8" x 8"

Blood Orange Square
Piecing Diagram

Sew an S9 strip to A; press seam toward A. Repeat to make four A-S9 strips.

Sew an A-S9 strip to opposite sides of the block centre; press seams toward the A-S9 strip.

Sew an S3 square to each end of each remaining A-S9 strip; press seams toward S3.

Sew the pieced strips to the remaining sides of the block centre to complete the pieced block; press seams away from the block centre.

Xtra Xtra

Skill Level

Beginner

Fabric & Piece Requirements

1 S8 coral print

4 S3 orange solid

4—2" x 2½" A blue check

2—1" x 6" B yellow dot

2—1" x 7" C yellow dot

2—1¼" x 7" D turquoise tonal

2—1¼" x 8½" E turquoise tonal

1—2" x 36" strip gold solid for binding

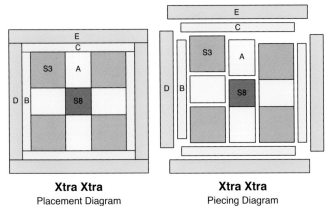

Xtra Xtra
Placement Diagram
8" x 8"

Xtra Xtra
Piecing Diagram

2—1" x 6" B red print

2—1" x 7" C red print

2—1¼" x 7" D blue check

2—1¼" x 8½" E blue check

1—2" x 36" strip red tonal for binding

Instructions

Sew A to opposite sides of S8 to make the centre row; press seams toward A.

Sew A between two S3 squares; press seams toward A. Repeat to make two A-S3 rows.

Sew an A-S3 row to opposite sides of the centre row; press seams toward the A-S3 rows.

Sew B to opposites sides, and then C to top and bottom of the pieced centre; press seams toward B and C.

Sew D to opposite sides, and then E to top and bottom of the pieced centre to complete the pieced block; press seams toward D and E.

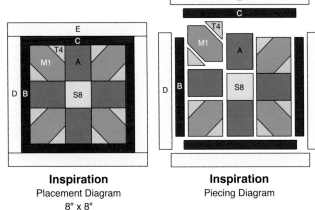

Inspiration
Placement Diagram
8" x 8"

Inspiration
Piecing Diagram

Instructions

Sew A to opposite sides of S8 to complete the centre row; press seams toward A.

Sew T4 to opposite sides of M1 to make an M-T unit; press seams toward T4. Repeat to make four M-T units.

Join two M-T units with A to make a side row; press seams toward A. Repeat to make two side rows.

Sew a side row to opposite sides of the centre row; press seams toward the centre row.

Sew B to opposite sides, and then C to top and bottom of the pieced centre; press seams toward B and C.

Sew D opposites sides, and then E to top and bottom of the pieced centre to complete the pieced block; press seams toward D and E.

Inspiration

Skill Level

Easy

Fabric & Piece Requirements

1 S8 blue solid

8 T4 lavender solid

4 M1 royal blue tonal

4—2" x 2½" A coral print

Hot Cross Bun

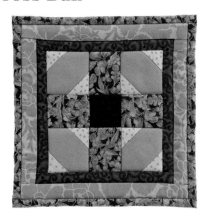

Skill Level

Easy

Fabric & Piece Requirements

1 S8 dark red print

8 T4 yellow dot

4 M1 lavender solid

4—2" x 2½" A red print

2—1" x 6" B royal blue tonal

2—1" x 7" C royal blue tonal

2—1¼" x 7" D orange tonal

2—1¼" x 8½" E orange tonal

1—2" x 36" strip red print for binding

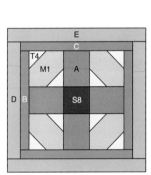

Hot Cross Bun
Placement Diagram
8" x 8"

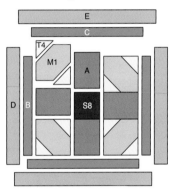

Hot Cross Bun
Piecing Diagram

Instructions

Piece referring to the instructions for Inspiration and to the Piecing Diagram for Hot Cross Bun to complete the pieced block.

Blue Cross

Skill Level

Easy

Fabric & Piece Requirements

4 S6 yellow print

4 M1 blue solid

8 T4 yellow print

4—1¼" x 4½" A coral print

2—1" x 6" B purple print

2—1" x 7" C purple print

2—1¼" x 7" D rust stripe

2—1¼" x 8½" E rust stripe

1—2" x 36" strip gold solid for binding

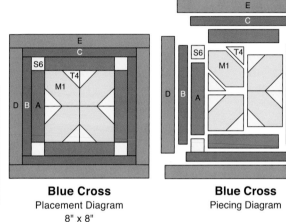

Blue Cross
Placement Diagram
8" x 8"

Blue Cross
Piecing Diagram

Instructions

Sew T4 to opposite sides of M1 to make an M-T unit; press seams toward T4. Repeat to make four M-T units.

Join two M-T units as shown in Figure 1; press seam in one direction. Repeat to make two units.

Figure 1

Join the M-T units to complete the block centre; press seam in one direction.

Sew A to opposite sides of the block centre; press seams toward A.

Sew S6 to each end of each remaining A; press seams toward A.

Sew an A-S6 unit to the top and bottom of the block centre; press seams toward A-S6.

Sew B to opposite sides, and then C to top and bottom of the pieced centre; press seams toward B and C.

Sew D opposite sides, and then E to top and bottom of the pieced centre to complete the pieced block; press seams toward D and E. ■

Dramatic Impact

Designs by Trice Boerens

The addition of black fabric makes the designs stand out in this set of theatrically named blocks.

Notes

Cut pieces as listed either using a rotary cutter and rotary ruler, or using the templates which start on page 46.

Refer to the General Instructions (see pages 2–4) for a list of basic sewing supplies and tools needed, and for instructions to finish your pot holders.

Refer to the Piecing Diagram given with each block for assembly ideas.

Gypsy Rose

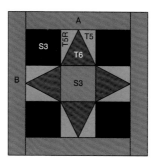

Gypsy Rose
Placement Diagram
8" x 8"

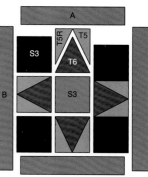

Gypsy Rose
Piecing Diagram

Sew a side unit to opposite sides of the floral S3 to make the centre row; press seams toward S3.

Sew a black S3 to each side of a side unit to make a side row; press seams away from the side unit. Repeat to make two side rows.

Sew the centre row between the side rows; press seams away from the centre row.

Sew A to the top and bottom, and B to opposite sides of the pieced centre; press seams toward A and B to complete the pieced block.

Stagestruck

Skill Level

Easy

Fabric & Piece Requirements

1 S3 floral

4 S3 black print

8 T5 black dot (reverse 4 for T5R)

4 T6 black floral

2—1½" x 6½" A rose tonal

2—1½" x 8½" B rose tonal

1—2" x 36" strip burgundy print for binding

Instructions

Sew T5 and T5R to T6 to make a side unit; press seams away from T6. Repeat to make four side units.

Skill Level

Intermediate

Fabric & Piece Requirements

1 S2 magenta mottled

4 S3 purple tonal

16 T5 white solid (reverse 8 for T5R)

8 T6 black floral

4 T7 black print

1—2" x 36" strip purple print for binding

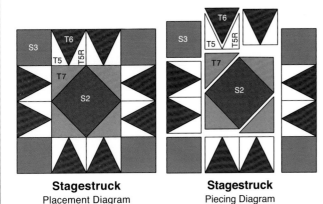

Stagestruck
Placement Diagram
8" x 8"

Stagestruck
Piecing Diagram

Instructions

Sew T7 to each side of S2 to complete the centre unit; press seams toward T7.

Sew T5 and T5R to T6 to complete a T unit; press seams away from T6. Repeat to make eight T units.

Join two T units to complete a side unit; press seam in one direction. Repeat to make four side units.

Sew a side unit to opposite sides of the centre unit to complete the centre row; press seams toward the centre unit.

Sew S3 to each end of each remaining side unit to make side rows; press seams toward S3.

Sew the side rows to opposite sides of the centre row to complete the pieced block; press seams toward the side rows.

Bright Lights

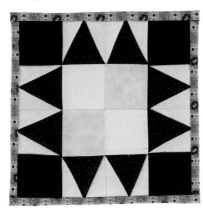

Skill Level

Intermediate

Fabric & Piece Requirements

2 S3 each white solid and peach mottled

4 S3 black solid

16 T5 cream tonal (reverse 8 for T5R)

8 T6 black print

1—2" x 36" strip rust mottled for binding

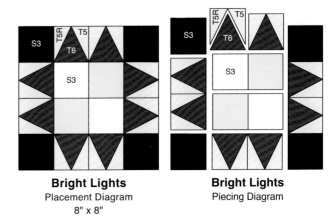

Bright Lights
Placement Diagram
8" x 8"

Bright Lights
Piecing Diagram

Instructions

Sew a white S3 to a peach S3; press seam toward darker fabric. Repeat to make two S3 rows.

Join the S3 rows to complete the block centre; press seam in one direction.

Sew T5 and T5R to T6 to complete a T unit; press seams away from T6. Repeat to make eight T units.

Join two T units to complete a side unit; press seam in one direction. Repeat to make four side units.

Sew a side unit to opposite sides of the centre unit to complete the centre row; press seams toward the centre unit.

Sew S3 to each end of each remaining side unit to make side rows; press seams toward S3.

Sew the side rows to opposite sides of the centre row to complete the pieced block; press seams toward the side rows.

Opening Night

Skill Level

Easy

Fabric & Piece Requirements

4 S3 black print

1 S4 black dot

4 T4 white dot

Dramatic Impact

8 T5 white dot (reverse 4 for T5R)

4 T6 black dot

2—1½" x 6½" A yellow print

2—1½" x 8½" B yellow print

1—2" x 36" strip rust mottled for binding

Instructions

Sew T4 to each side of S4 to complete the centre unit; press seams toward T4.

Sew T5 and T5R to T6 to complete a side unit; press seams away from T6. Repeat to make four side units.

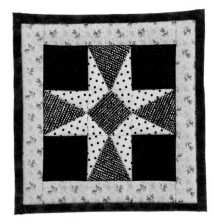

Skill Level
Intermediate

Fabric & Piece Requirements
5 S4 black dot

20 T4 white dot

8 T5 grey mottled (reverse 4 for T5R)

4 T6 black solid

6—1" x 2½" A grey print

2—1" x 7½" B grey print

2—1" x 7½" C cream tonal

2—1" x 8½" D cream tonal

1—2" x 36" strip black solid for binding

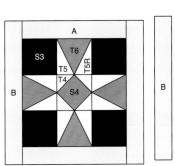

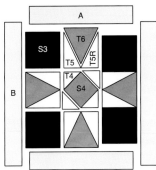

Opening Night
Placement Diagram
8" x 8"

Opening Night
Piecing Diagram

Sew a side unit to opposite sides of the centre unit to complete the centre row; press seams toward the centre unit.

Sew S3 to opposite sides of each remaining side unit to make side rows; press seams toward S3.

Sew a side row to opposite sides of the centre row; press seams toward side rows.

Sew A to the top and bottom, and B to opposite sides of the pieced rows to complete the pieced block; press seams toward A and B.

Repertory Group

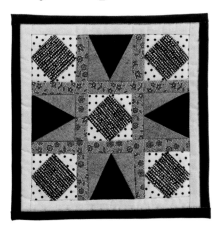

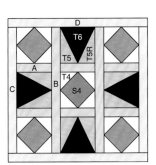
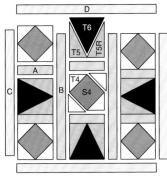

Repertory Group
Placement Diagram
8" x 8"

Repertory Group
Piecing Diagram

Instructions

Sew T4 to each side of S4 to complete an S4 unit; press seams toward T4. Repeat to make five S4 units.

Sew T5 and T5R to T6 to complete a T unit; press seams away from T6. Repeat to make four T units.

Join one T unit, two S4 units and two A strips to complete a side row; press seams toward A. Repeat to make two side rows.

Join one S4 unit with two T units and two A strips to complete the centre row; press seams toward A.

Join the side and centre rows with B to complete the pieced centre; press seams toward B.

Sew C to opposite sides and D to the top and bottom of the pieced centre to complete the pieced block; press seams toward C and D.

Walk of Fame
Skill Level
Intermediate

Fabric & Piece Requirements

3 S4 black floral

12 T4 black dot

12 T5 white dot (reverse 6 for T5R)

6 T6 black dot

2—1½" x 6½" A black floral

2—1½" x 8½" B black floral

1—2" x 36" strip wine solid for binding

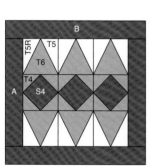

Walk of Fame
Placement Diagram
8" x 8"

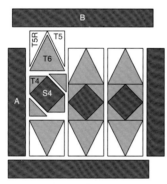

Walk of Fame
Piecing Diagram

Instructions

Sew T4 to each side of S4 to complete an S4 unit; press seams toward T4. Repeat to make three S4 units.

Sew T5 and T5R to T6 to complete a T unit; press seams away from T6. Repeat to make 6 T units.

Sew a T unit to opposite sides of an S4 unit to complete one row; repeat to make three rows. Press seams of one row toward the T units, and of two rows toward the S4 unit.

Join the rows, alternating seam pressing to complete the pieced centre; press seams in one direction.

Sew A to opposite sides and B to the top and bottom of the pieced centre to complete the pieced block; press seams toward A and B.

Highs & Lows

Skill Level

Intermediate

Fabric & Piece Requirements

16 T5 each grey mottled and black print (reverse 8 of each for T5R)

8 T6 each black solid and grey print

1—2" x 36" strip pink stripe for binding

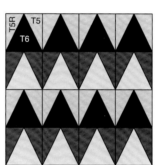

Highs & Lows
Placement Diagram
8" x 8"

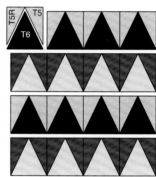

Highs & Lows
Piecing Diagram

Instructions

Sew a black T5 and T5R to a grey print T6 to make a grey T unit; press seams away from T6. Repeat to make eight each grey and black T units.

Join four grey T units to make a grey row; press seams in one direction. Repeat to make two grey rows.

Join four black T units to make a black row; press seams in one direction. Repeat to make two black rows.

Arrange and join the rows referring to the Piecing Diagram to complete the pieced block; press seams in one direction. ■

Appliqué & Piecing Templates

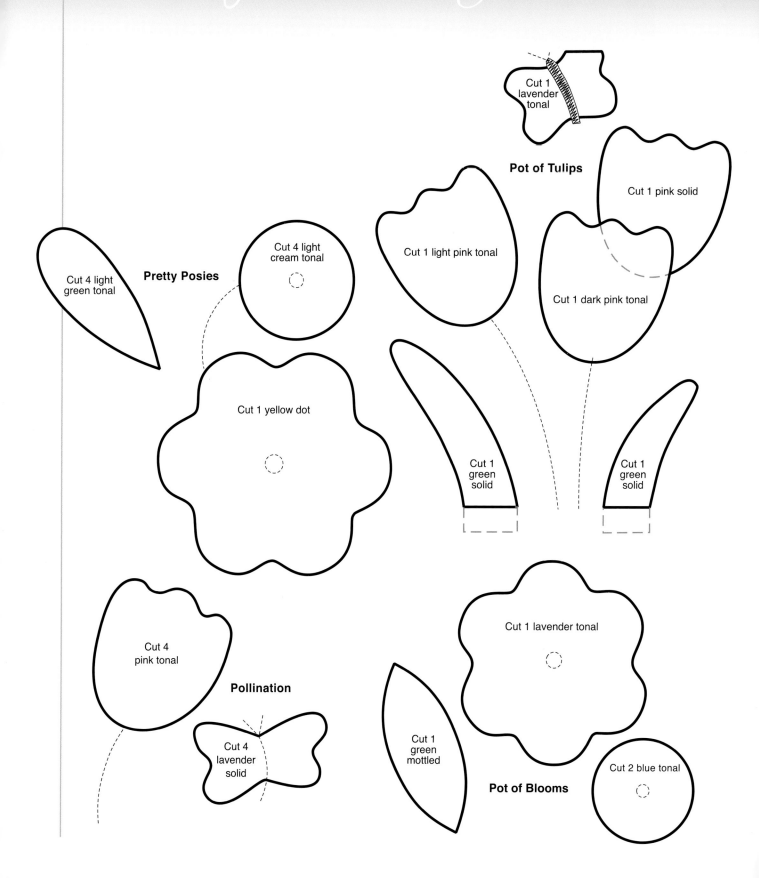

Cut 1 lavender tonal

Pot of Tulips

Cut 1 pink solid

Cut 1 light pink tonal

Cut 1 dark pink tonal

Pretty Posies

Cut 4 light cream tonal

Cut 4 light green tonal

Cut 1 yellow dot

Cut 1 green solid

Cut 1 green solid

Cut 4 pink tonal

Pollination

Cut 4 lavender solid

Cut 1 lavender tonal

Cut 1 green mottled

Pot of Blooms

Cut 2 blue tonal

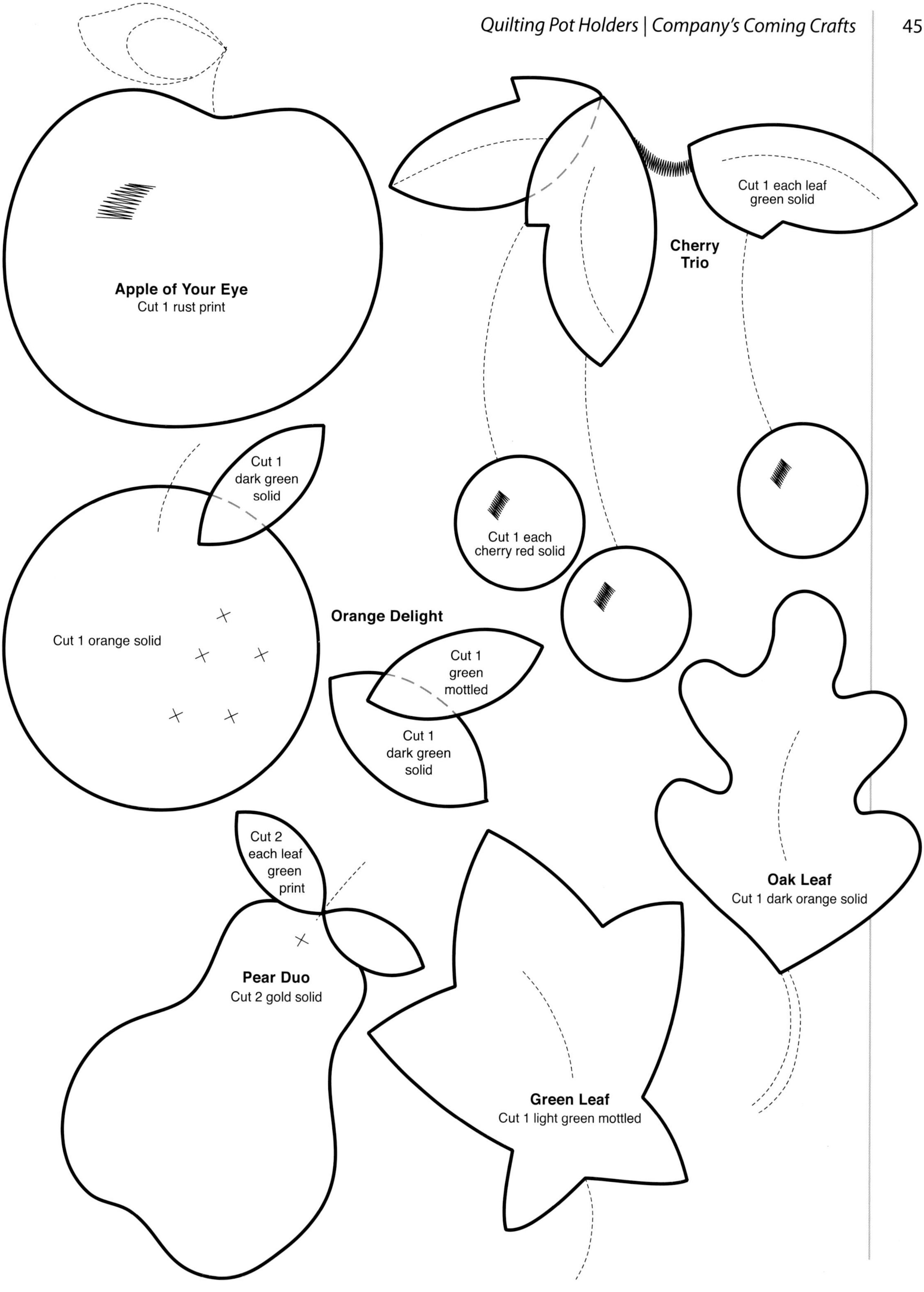

Apple of Your Eye
Cut 1 rust print

Cherry Trio

Cut 1 each leaf
green solid

Cut 1
dark green
solid

Cut 1 orange solid

Orange Delight

Cut 1 each
cherry red solid

Cut 1
green
mottled

Cut 1
dark green
solid

Oak Leaf
Cut 1 dark orange solid

Cut 2
each leaf
green print

Pear Duo
Cut 2 gold solid

Green Leaf
Cut 1 light green mottled

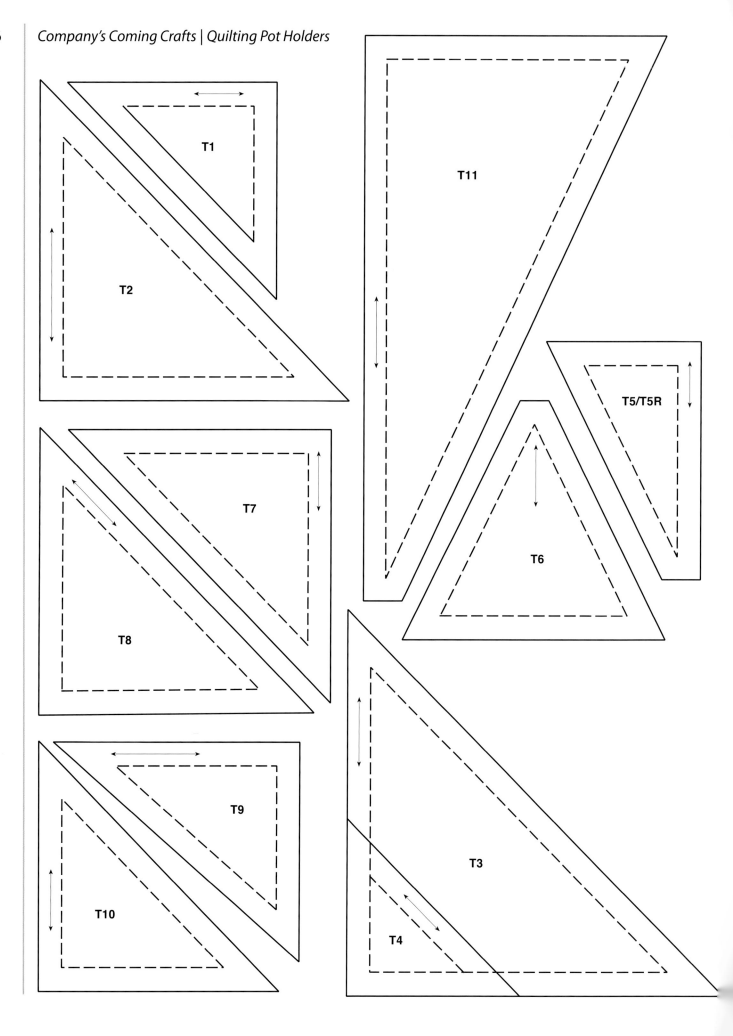

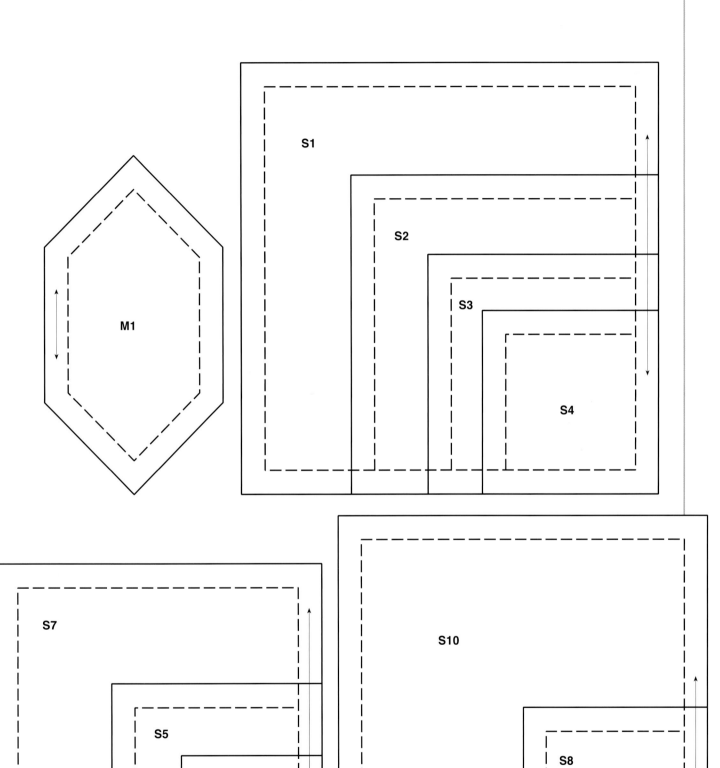

Embroidery Stitches

Satin Stitch

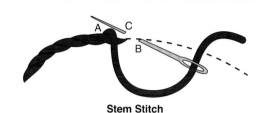

Stem Stitch

Straight Stitch

Metric Conversion Charts

METRIC CONVERSIONS

yards	x	.9144	=	metres (m)
yards	x	91.44	=	centimetres (cm)
inches	x	2.54	=	centimetres (cm)
inches	x	25.40	=	millimetres (mm)
inches	x	.0254	=	metres (m)

centimetres	x	.3937	=	inches
metres	x	1.0936	=	yards

INCHES INTO MILLIMETRES & CENTIMETRES (Rounded off slightly)

inches	mm	cm	inches	cm	inches	cm	inches	cm
1/8	3	0.3	5	12.5	21	53.5	38	96.5
1/4	6	0.6	51/2	14	22	56	39	99
3/8	10	1	6	15	23	58.5	40	101.5
1/2	13	1.3	7	18	24	61	41	104
5/8	15	1.5	8	20.5	25	63.5	42	106.5
3/4	20	2	9	23	26	66	43	109
7/8	22	2.2	10	25.5	27	68.5	44	112
1	25	2.5	11	28	28	71	45	114.5
11/4	32	3.2	12	30.5	29	73.5	46	117
11/2	38	3.8	13	33	30	76	47	119.5
13/4	45	4.5	14	35.5	31	79	48	122
2	50	5	15	38	32	81.5	49	124.5
21/2	65	6.5	16	40.5	33	84	50	127
3	75	7.5	17	43	34	86.5		
31/2	90	9	18	46	35	89		
4	100	10	19	48.5	36	91.5		
41/2	115	11.5	20	51	37	94		

Quilting Pot Holders

First Printing August 2011

Library and Archives Canada Cataloguing in Publication
Quilting pot holders.
(Pattern book series)
ISBN 978-1-897477-41-0
1. Quilting--Patterns. 2. Potholders.
I. Series: Pattern book series
TT835.Q5466 2010   746.46'043   C2009-907411-7

Published by
Company's Coming Publishing Limited
2311-96 Street
Edmonton, Alberta, Canada T6N 1G3
Tel: 780-450-6223 Fax: 780-450-1857
www.companyscoming.com

Company's Coming is a registered trademark owned by Company's Coming Publishing Limited

Printed in China